Lojong Poems

Lojong Poems

reflections
on the path

marga ret
with artwork by
david crouch

Bird of Paradise Press
Lexington, Virginia

ISBN: 978-1-7347823-7-0
Library of Congress Control Number: 2022948001

Bird of Paradise Press
1223 N. Lee Hwy, #250
Lexington, VA 24450
birdofparadisepress.org

Front cover design and interior layout
by Annie Heckman.

table of contents

Breathing out
I send clear light to all beings
breathing in
I receive all suffering
slowly breathing out and in
I find calm abiding, clarity and joy
I ride the precious air that gives me life
without asking anything for this gift,
and so I give joy, happiness, relief in return
for my equanimity.

dedication

This work is dedicated to the memory of my
beloved husband, David G. Crouch, and to the
loving memory of the 14th Shamar Rinpoche,
our very great teacher and friend. It could not
have come to fruition without their presence
in my heart-mind as well as the power of their
personal guidance and encouragement.

My deepest wish is that these poetic
reflections will honor their lives and work,
their wisdom and compassion for all beings,
and that the highest good of all life may
manifest in all its joyful expression.

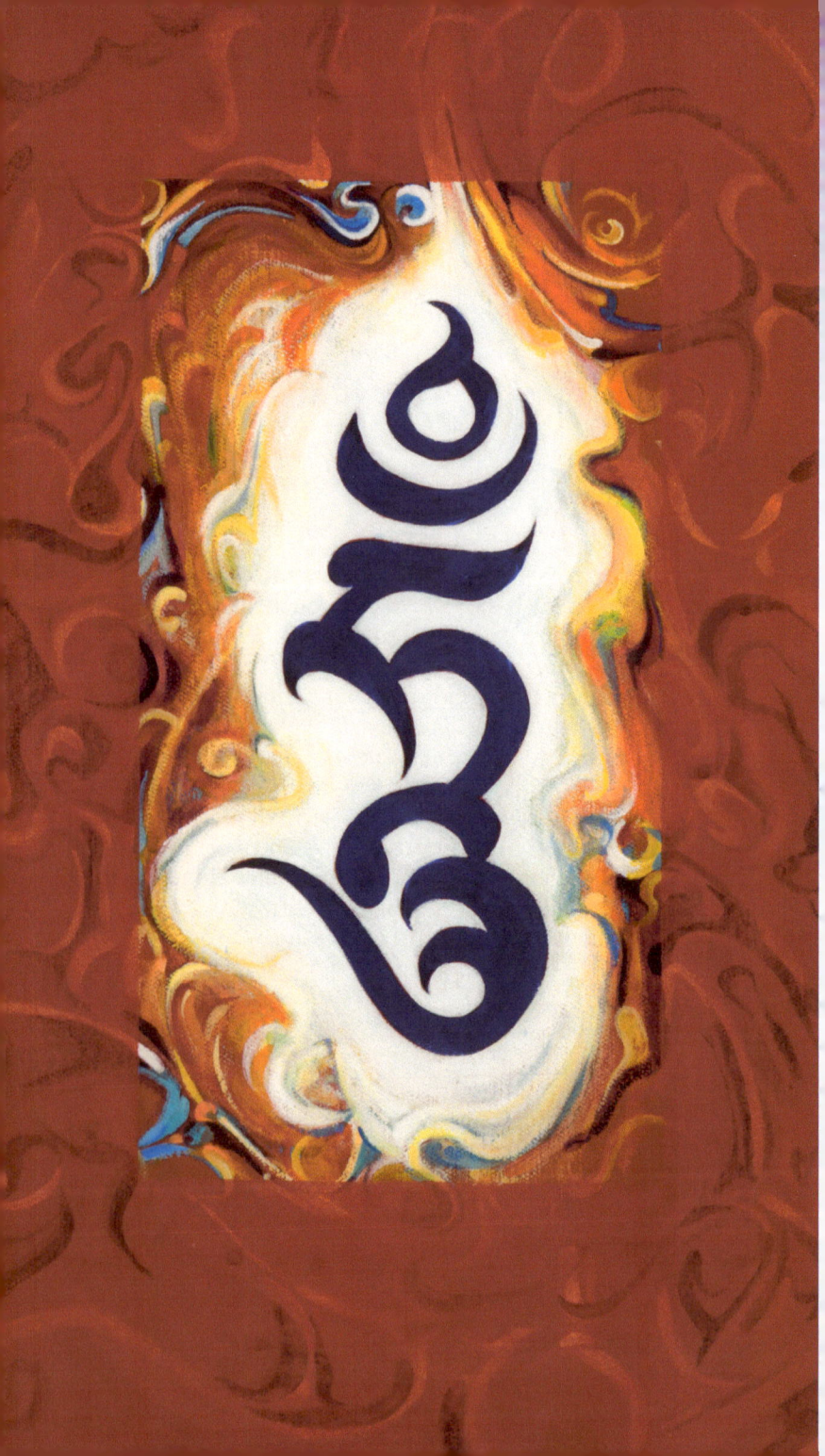

publisher's note

The team at Bird of Paradise Press was so happy to be introduced to this collection of poetry from longtime Dharma student and friend of the press, Marga Ret (Crouch). The introduction led to this project, an opportunity to deliver special, original material to appreciative readers. In these poems, Marga Ret uses Buddhist *lojong* slogans, a famous group of Buddhist teachings, for inspiration and structure; the slogans were originally translated for inclusion in the book *The Path to Awakening* by Marga Ret's teacher and Tibetan Buddhist lineage holder, the 14th Shamar Rinpoche (1952–2014). To accompany all the slogans, Marga Ret has composed poems that create an avenue for readers to sink into the slogans and stay with them. Both the slogans and the corresponding poetry have been included in this book.

To provide some background, *lojong*, the teachings known as "mind training" (Tibetan: *lojong*) are a profound system of contemplative practices that helps bring mindfulness, awareness, and insight to our experiences, both on and off the meditation cushion. These teachings have been preserved by an unbroken lineage of masters since the time of the Buddha, and were considered particularly helpful for modern-day practitioners by the 14th Shamar Rinpoche. The root text with commentary can be found in the book by Shamar Rinpoche, *The Path to Awakening* (Delphinium Books, distributed by Harper Collins, 2014).

The press was equally friendly with Marga Ret's husband, David Crouch (1933–2017), a remarkable artist who integrated Dharma practice with his art to produce unique pieces, many of which were enjoyed by Shamar Rinpoche during his lifetime. Some of the resulting pieces are featured in this book.

It is not an accident that Marga Ret has the rare qualifications needed to compose the poetry featured here. For decades, Marga Ret and David followed the guidance of their teacher, starting with one of Rinpoche's first talks in the United States in Santa Barbara, California. Over the years, Marga Ret and David, along with many students at the time, learned directly from their teacher as he taught about *lojong*, and saw his book *The Path to Awakening* completed and published many years after they had already been practicing the slogans according to Rinpoche's instructions. They also engaged in countless programs of authentic Tibetan Buddhist studies and practices held by lamas and Dharma teachers who were trained by Shamar Rinpoche. In the process, Marga Ret has grown to be a mature and meticulous student of the Dharma. She has always applied her sharp mind to Dharma, the same mind that she employed to earn a PhD in Musicology. We are now the beneficiaries of her poetry, which is part of the fruits of her years of Buddhist study, practice, and contemplation.

We hope that readers enjoy reading the poetry and benefit from the teachings within. May we all feel a little more immersed in the precious *lojong* teachings.

preface

It is with great respect and deep humility that I thank the 14th Shamar Rinpoche for his translation and commentary *The Path to Awakening*, which is used here as a basis for these poetic reflections on *lojong*.

I also thank all the spiritual teachers, guides, and friends in the Bodhi Path sangha who listened to and encouraged the creation of these poems. It would not have happened without your presence in my heart-mind.

References used for my own practice, and study guides in these poetic reflections, are

- *The Great Path of Awakening* by Jamgön Kongtrul, translated by Ken McLeod;
- *Enlightened Courage* by Dilgo Khyentse Rinpoche, translated by the Padmakara Translation Group;
- *Training the Mind and Cultivating Loving-Kindness* by Chögyam Trungpa Rinpoche, edited by Judith L. Lief; and

- *The Path to Awakening*, written by my teacher, the 14th Shamar Rinpoche, edited and translated by Lara Braitstein.

I bow to the vast wisdom of all the teachers I have encountered on the path to awakening. May their wisdom and compassion enter the mind-stream of all who hear their words, to hold in their heart-mind on this incredible journey. May it be of benefit to all beings.

Marga Ret
(Karma Yeshe Lhamo,
Bodhisattvayāna refuge vow and name
given by the 14th Shamar Rinpoche, 2000)

Learn the Preliminaries;
furthermore, be trained in not
conceptualizing the three spheres.

Quiet mind
holds brilliant light
embracing all
prepare to be
renouncing all
let go of nothing
no need to cling
embrace the guru
and the blessing.

Empty nature
is the gift
contemplating worldly things
the four dissatisfactions
karma here
all structures are unstable
causes and effects
gestate in seven-pointed ease
water and clouds prepare.

I

(I)
First, train in the preliminaries;
think that all phenomena are like a dream.

Slowing down, seeing
I notice distraction and attraction
at play.

and

Wax and brush, color and ink
hard bone, soft tissue
multiple designs.

second point

Key instructions for training in the two bodhicittas, beginning with ultimate bodhicitta.

The ultimate, the relative
giving all
no holding out
no holding on
connecting disconnects
a momentary gap, clear glimpse
of nothing
both the same.

First, begin with ultimate bodhicitta
to develop conventional bodhicitta correctly.

(2)
Analyze the unborn nature of mind.

Moon cloud silhouettes the tree,
silken leaves and branches —
rain rides the wind.

(3)

Purify the strongest negative emotion first.

Shining light on fear
dispels many shadows
before they take effect.

(4)
Even the remedy naturally liberates itself.

Let go!
the bow bends, the arrow yearns
flickering in the quickened air . . .

(5)
Rest in the essence of mind,
the basis of everything.

Negativities bloom —
freedom soars . . .
the essence of each is empty.

(6)

In post-meditation, know that all
phenomena are illusory.

Phenomena arise,
the day is seen as real —
the trickster misleads.

(7)
Abandon all hope for results.

Hope and Fear bring false security...
ego's sneak attack
drags downward.

Second, the instructions on training in the union of conventional and ultimate bodhicitta.

(8)
**Practice alternately the two,
giving and taking.**

> Practice and view
> together bear fruit...
> compassion dissolves illusion.

Place the two upon the breath.

The alchemist transmutes the suffering
breathe out and in . . .
I for You.

(10)
Three objects, three poisons,
three roots of virtue.

Objects lure,
three poisons beguile —
a well-intentioned life corrects.

II

Train your conduct by means
of the slogans.

·

These pith slogans
bring order to the day and night
of our dilemma.

third point

Convert adversities into
the path of awakening.

This old reality rarely shows its other face
we engage the play
to heighten the old way.

Opaque drifts and bubbles
crush and hold aloft some shreds
of fading images.

Dark and light illuminate
the other side the view within
surrounding and extending in clear light.

Among ordinary and extraordinary
instructions, begin with the first:

(12)
When beings and the world are
filled with evil, convert adversities
into the path of awakening.

> Self-clinging, negative actions
> become the path
> to liberation.

> *and*

> No secrets here!
> no impure karma seedlings —
> all joy is outward bound.

Second, among the three extraordinary instructions, the first is how conventional bodhicitta is used to convert adversities into the path of awakening:

(13)
**Hold one fault accountable
for all misfortunes.**

Ego-cherishing,
selfish actions never end . . .
the blame belongs here.

Reflect on the great kindness of all beings.

Abandon your revenge —
relinquish ego . . .
reap a deeper harvest.

*The second is how ultimate bodhicitta is used
to transform adversities into the path of
awakening:*

(15)
Cultivate deluded
appearance as the Four Kayas;
Emptiness is the unsurpassed protection.

The vast display fades,
uncovers modes of experience —
subtle truth.

and

The winter of illusion is hard
why wait for spring
when now is here …

(16)
Three views are like the treasury
of the sky, the unsurpassed
protection of the yoga.

Befriend adversity —
all obstacles become
three views of merit.

and

As views defeat the harm
each moment transforms
to awakened nature.

The third is the extraordinary instruction to
convert adversities into the path of awakening:

(17)
Mastering
the four practices
is the supreme method.

Develop, refrain,
welcome, give —
this unjust world shows its sacred face.

(18)
Whatever you encounter in the present,
use it in your meditation.

Joy and pain are one
in giving and taking ...
compassion makes it so.

fourth point
Implement Mind Training in this life.

In mirrors we recede
grow smaller and yet multiply
we see ourselves
too sure of being seen
our tiny hatreds spawn
one mirror breaks
the pieces fall
in sharp articulating streams
to etch our lives
from high to low
no meaning, no non-meaning
while the splinters forge
the mirror of mind.

(19)
The instructions condensed
into their essence:
Train in the five powers.

Secure in lovingkindness
unchanging virtue
empowers all life.

The Great Vehicle teachings on death
are the five powers themselves;
your conduct is critical.

Designed to die
how then may I think of my own Self
as immortal . . .

and

How beautiful they are
the clouds coming to greet me
to guide me home . . .

The palace doors are open
bright ruby iridescent
royal way. . .

Striker and bowl are one
singing down the corridors
the way I came. . .

Autumn moon cloud drift fades
crimson brilliance blinds
swaying reeds move aside. . .

fifth point
The Measure of Mind Training.

I was weak
but my weakness
became strength

I was unwanted
but my unwantedness
became love for others

I was unlovely
but my unloveliness
became great beauty

I was jealous
but my jealousy
became rejoicing

I was angry
but my anger
became like water

I was proud
but my pride
became enriching

I was passionate
but passion
became joy in giving

I was ignorant
but ignorance dissolved
becoming naked space

The tiger is awakened,
focused and determined

Now I ride the tiger.

21

All dharma teachings are
for a single purpose.

The mango tree blossoms
its fruit is pure and sweet—
wake up—pluck it now!

(22)
**Rely on the better
of the two witnesses.**

You there—leave now!
get out of your own way
as you hover within clouds.

Be sustained continuously
by a joyful mind.

Fearlessness
knowing what is, admitting confusion —
the fruit is joy.

(24)
You are well trained if you can even
withstand distraction.

Catastrophe calls,
the abyss is there, no safety net—
leap across!

sixth point

Commitments of Mind Training.

Two thousand ways to describe the seasons—
Only one way to live.

Eighty-four thousand teachings—
Only one is necessary.

Ten thousand things to know—
Only the present moment matters.

Eighteen doors of perception—
One fruit, one taste.

(25)
Always abide by the
three basic principles.

Abide in humility—
body, speech, mind...
a single way of life.

(26)
Remaining natural, transform
your attitude.

Discretion matters...
internal antidotes
without external show.

(27)
Do not talk about
the defects of others.

Honoring all beings,
contemplate the grace of life...
a jewel unseen.

(28)
**Whatever the faults of others may be,
do not contemplate them.**

Noticing and pointing
creates a lingering sadness
for beings.

(29)
Abandon
poisonous food.

At the Empowerment
did you hear the three jewels
and the orchids?

(30)

**Helping others is not
based on returning favors.**

Put aside attitudes!
take a chance for once—
avoid the dead-end rule.

(31)
Do not expose the faults
of others to irritate them.

Mind's nature unborn,
virtuous beyond reference
abandons judging...

(32)
Do not
wait in ambush.

Give up your planned attack!
rely instead
on awakening heart-mind.

(33)
Never strike at the heart.

Hoping for the bad luck of others
to bear fruit
traps both parties.

Do not put an ox's load on a cow.

Mean spirited tactics of blame
are flawed...
align the three doors quickly!

(35)
Do not aim to be the best.

Don't tell me...let me guess
you're enlightened—
or so you hoped a while back.

and

The race to be the best or...
sincerity in practice...
make the choice.

Do not misuse the remedy.

Placing yourself above,
pretending benevolence,
the noose tightens...

(37)
Do not use gods for evil.

Tear it down!
ecstatic self-hypnosis
builds the opposite effect.

(38)
Be like a humble servant before all.

Self-interest demeans—
purity and simplicity
stand the test.

(39)
Do not delight in the suffering of others.

Wishing injury on others
is using a short sword
on yourself.

seventh point
Advice for Mind Training

Unborn, a whisper yet unrecognized
luminescent purity is carried
by the light of ancient stars.

At play, the worldly traps arise
novelties surprise and beckon imitation
pretence to delight.

At rest, three thousand candles
flicker unadorned
the glowing sound is white.

57

(40)
Practice all yogas in one way.

On and off the cushion
maintain transcendent view
to help all others.

(41)
Subdue all obstacles by one method.

Accomplish the practice—
remember others
through your own suffering.

(42)
Two actions to perform:
at the beginning and at the end.

Through all your days and nights
let each moment of practice and mind
be one.

**Be patient with whichever
of the two arises.**

Ebb and flow,
only change is constant...
to stay in balance is the key.

(44)
Guard the two
even at the cost of your life.

Essential vows,
the bonds of ultimate protection—
keep them with you.

and

Be settled in mind—
don't talk to the wind of
causes and conditions.

Roots exposed, old trees die...
the garden enriched,
the lotus bides its time.

and

Look deeply within, avoid self-clinging...
find the well-spring
of wisdom.

(46)
Keep the three main causes.

The teacher leads gently
train yourself along the path—
be practical.

Cultivate the three without diminishment.

Why linger in malaise...
commitment becomes
heroic energy.

(48)
Make the three inseparable.

Not three but one!
engage determination...
the cloudless sky is vast.

Practice with impartiality.

Think beyond the bias
and warp—
weave new patterns of experience.

(50)
All training must be pervasive and
profound.

Mind's presence,
illusive and intangible—
no time to miss the mark.

(51)
Meditate consistently in every circumstance.

Conditions and terms
arise as food for thoughts…
practice alleviates.

(52)
Do not depend on external conditions.

Great potential lives
in adversity...
how could it be otherwise?

(53)

From now on, practice is the chief priority.

Catch hold! The raft floats by
to carry you over
to the other side...

(54)
Do not be misdirected.

Positive intentions
virtuous actions...
the way of skillful means.

(55)
Do not be inconsistent.

When the mind is troubled
hurrying, you fall behind
and lose the way.

(56)
Train uninterruptedly.

Passions subside
the effort is noble...
reflections of a jeweled net.

Liberate by examination and analysis.

Don't be thrown off!
scrutinize the past,
grounded in the present moment.

(58)
Do not seek recognition.

Restraint begins with not expecting—
the diamond gathers light
to give...

Do not hold on to anger.

Hunger of anger,
hunger of compassion—
feed one or the other.

(60)
Do not be moody.

Know ignorance well...
to discipline the mind
the jewel is in the heart.

(61)
Do not seek gratitude.

The singing bowl is heard in valleys
across rivers
asking nothing.

and

The wild bird sings with no
reward for its song...
giving, it flies away.

notes on process

I designed these poems with the hope that they might be useful in various ways: by practitioners for individual meditation support and reflection, by counselors and therapists in their work, and as a companion to the 14th Shamar Rinpoche's commentary The Path to Awakening (Delphinium Books, 2014) on The Seven Points of Mind Training, a Tibetan text compiled in the twelfth century by Chekawa Yeshe Dorje (1101–1175).

The traditional *lojong* text has seven points, followed by numbered slogans. I have written seven long poems, one for each point, and the beginning standalone poem, which is an expression of tonglen, giving and taking, in which one's meditation is focused on breathing in the suffering of all beings and breathing out to them the clear light of awakening and relief from their suffering.

This *lojong* text has been in use as a personal transformative practice by people from all walks of life since its inception. Each of the seven points is followed by short slogans that encourage the practitioner to look inward deeply to discover possibilities for change, and then to cultivate changes in attitude and behavior. In so doing, the practice becomes a path to awakening that provides a way out of the confusion that defines so much of our conditioned existence. The 'Seven Points of Mind Training' have long been a venue for Buddhist masters and qualified teachers to engage in writing commentaries to enhance their own teaching, and to give support to practitioners, consequently, the number of slogans varies with each writer.

The 14th Shamar Rinpoche included 61 slogans, and I have adhered to his wisdom in creating these haiku.

The poetic structure in this collection is my own convention. I chose not to use the traditional 5–7–5 structure of Japanese haiku because my intention was to create intuitive poetry that was related to the quoted slogan, and so my motivation and intention were to address that slogan. However, each one of my haiku does have seventeen syllables, three lines, very little punctuation, and no title. I also realized, as the writing began, that the English language in this context allowed me the range of flexibility necessary to express the possibility of looking inward to recognition and change instead of outward to well-established thought patterns and egoic expectations.

I began the project in 2012 and completed it in the spring of 2014. At first my reaction to the teaching of mind training was that I didn't really want to live my life by slogans; however, I knew that personal transformation, although not easy, was a much better way to live than to steep in a confused state of mind, so I chose to write myself out of confusion in this way. My intention was to create a haiku for each slogan. This sometimes led to two or more haiku on the same slogan. This process helped me to work with them in a broader way, and to enjoy the result of transforming my own negative emotions into emotional clarity and strength. This soon became a way of life that helped me to make changes in my own attitude that gradually became a way to be supportive of friends, family, and colleagues, resulting in a healthy and happy move away from criticism, advice, opinions, and judgements.

david glenn (judd) crouch
1933–2017

David's career spanned some 60 years, in two
major areas: as an active exhibiting studio
artist, and as a master scientific illustrator for
the University of California, Santa Barbara.
He was awarded a Master of Arts degree from
San Diego State University. Upon moving to
Santa Barbara, David was an active member
of the Santa Barbara Art Association. His
work is in private collections and professional
publications worldwide. His philosophy was
"The image is behind the eyes, the line is
already there."

marga ret
1937–

Margaret L. Crouch (pen name "Marga Ret") holds a PhD in Musicology, University of California, Santa Barbara and two performance degrees: in piano (San Diego State University), and harpsichord (UC Santa Barbara). She and her husband, David, were devoted to Buddhist practice and to the 14th Shamar Rinpoche and the Bodhi Path centers founded by Shamar Rinpoche.

www.ingramcontent.com/pod-product-compliance
Lightning Source LLC
Chambersburg PA
CBHW041958090426
42811CB00026B/1928/J